The Wooden Horse

The Fall of Troy

Written by I. M. Richardson
Illustrated by Hal Frenck

Troll Associates

Library of Congress Cataloging in Publication Data

Richardson, I. M.
    The wooden horse.

    Summary: A retelling of how the Greeks overcame the
Trojans with the aid of a wooden horse.
    [1. Mythology, Greek] I. Homer. II. Frenck, Hal, ill.
III. Title.
PZ8.1.R390Wo 1984   [883]   83-18061
ISBN 0-8167-0057-5 (lib. bdg.)
ISBN 0-8167-0058-3 (pbk.)

High on Mount Olympus, three goddesses were arguing. Athena, Aphrodite, and Hera each wanted a beautiful golden apple bearing the words *For the Fairest*. Hera turned to her husband—Zeus, the most powerful god of all—and said, "Tell the others that I am the fairest." But Zeus knew that if he chose Hera, the other goddesses would be angry. So he said, "Go to Mount Ida, and let Paris make the judgement. He is as good a judge of beauty as anyone."

Paris was tending his flocks when the three goddesses approached him. Each of them tried to win his favor by offering him special gifts. Hera offered him power and wealth. Athena promised him knowledge and strength. But Aphrodite promised him love. "The most beautiful woman on earth shall fall in love with you," she said. "All you have to do is say that I am the fairest goddess of all."

Paris made his decision—he chose Aphrodite as the fairest goddess. Then he waited for Aphrodite to fulfill her promise. The most beautiful woman in the world was Helen, the lovely queen of Sparta. Although Helen was already married to Menelaos, the Spartan king, Paris knew that Aphrodite could make anything happen.

Paris went to Sparta to visit the king and queen. Menelaos greeted him warmly, for it was the custom to treat each guest like a close friend. But Aphrodite, the goddess of love, made Helen fall in love with Paris. As soon as Menelaos turned his back, Paris and Helen ran away together. They sailed across the Aegean Sea to the distant city of Troy.

Menelaos vowed to bring back his wife. He called on all the
other Greek kings to join him in a great war against Troy.
Soon, a mighty fleet left the shores of Greece and went off
to the Trojan War. They never dreamed that ten long years
later they would still be fighting the same war.

The great city of Troy was surrounded by a mighty wall. No matter what the Greeks did, they could not get inside. So they set up a huge camp between the city and the sea. For nine years, the Greeks battled the Trojans. First one side seemed to be winning, and then the other side seemed to have the upper hand. Then the luck would change again.

In the tenth year of the war, the Greeks and Trojans lost their greatest warriors. Hector, who was the brother of Paris, was killed by Achilles. Then Achilles, the greatest of the Greek warriors, was killed by Paris. Paris, in turn, was killed—but still neither side could claim victory.

The Greeks were more determined than ever to destroy Troy. "There must be some way we can get inside the city gates," said Odysseus. Odysseus was the King of Ithaca, and one of the cleverest men in all of Greece. "We must build a wooden horse," he decided. "It must be large enough for our greatest warriors to hide inside."

10

The work was begun at once. A huge platform was made, on which the horse would stand. Then a skilled woodcarver began shaping the horse's head and neck, as well as its feet and legs. From the distant walls of Troy, the Trojans could not see what was going on in the Greek camp.

The body of the horse was hollow. It had room enough to hold twenty Greek warriors, plus all their armor and weapons. There was even a secret trap door. The door was so well disguised that when it was closed, no one would ever have guessed it was there.

When the horse's head and neck had been carefully carved, they were fitted onto the horse's body. At last, the huge wooden horse was finished. It looked like a statue of a mighty war horse. "It is a perfect offering for Athena, the goddess of wisdom and war," said Odysseus. "Now it is time to put the rest of my plan into action."

Twenty of the best Greek warriors were chosen. Among them were Menelaos and the crafty Odysseus. If they failed, they would be killed by the Trojans. But if they succeeded, Troy would be burned to the ground. That night, the twenty men hid inside the horse. The trap door was closed tightly behind them.

The rest of the Greek army broke camp and set sail in their ships. As the sun rose, the Trojans looked out across the battlefield. Clearly, it seemed that the Greeks had given up. They had deserted their camp and left for home. Even now, their sails could be seen disappearing over the distant horizon.

On the plains outside Troy stood the mighty wooden horse. Was it a peace offering from the defeated Greeks? Or was it a secret weapon that would break through the gates? "This must be a trick of some kind," said an old Trojan priest. "I do not trust the Greeks when they leave gifts."

But the people began to celebrate what seemed to be a Trojan victory. They threw open the gates and rushed outside, rejoicing. The long, bitter war had finally ended! The people explored the ruins of the Greek camp, and they gathered around the huge wooden horse.

"Get back!" cried the old priest. "Can't you see that this is a trick?" Then some of the people said, "Perhaps the old priest is right." Others cried, "No! If this is a peace offering from the Greeks, we should bring it inside." But someone else shouted, "Let's burn it to ashes right where it stands!"

The twenty Greek soldiers knew what would happen if the horse were to be set on fire. But they could hear more and more Trojans saying, "Bring the horse inside!" Suddenly there was a hollow sound. The old priest had hurled a spear at the side of the horse. "Did you hear that?" he cried. "The horse is hollow inside!"

But Odysseus had thought of everything. At that very moment, a Greek soldier stumbled forth, his hands tied behind him. "Take pity on me," he cried. "My own countrymen tried to kill me before they set sail, but I escaped. They planned to offer me as a sacrifice to the gods—to guarantee themselves a speedy journey home." The Trojans saw his tears, and they believed his story.

Then the soldier told them about the wooden horse. "It is a
tribute to the goddess Athena," he said. "Odysseus hoped
you would burn it, for that would bring Athena's anger
down upon your city. He purposely made the horse too big
to fit through the gates of Troy. He feared that if you took it
inside the city walls, Athena would smile upon Troy instead
of Greece."

"It is a trick!" cried the old priest. "Do not listen to those lies." But as he spoke, two huge and terrible serpents came out of the sea. They slithered up onto the beach and headed straight toward the old priest. Then they coiled themselves around the old man, squeezing the life out of him.

"This must be a warning from the gods," cried the Trojans.
"If we destroy the horse, as the priest wanted us to do, our
fate will be the same as his!" Then they set about the difficult
task of getting the huge wooden horse into the city. They had
to take down part of the wall to do it. Then they dragged the
horse inside and rebuilt the wall.

A huge victory celebration was held. The Trojans had survived ten long years of battle against the mighty Greeks. Now was a time for feasting and merriment. Sentries were no longer needed at the top of the city walls or along the shore-line. So they joined the celebration.

It was late at night when the Trojans finally went to sleep. Then the Greek soldier went to the wooden horse and opened the secret trap door. Out slipped the Greek warriors who had been hiding inside. Odysseus was first, followed by Menelaos and the others. Their helmets and shields reflected the soft glow of the moonlight.

Odysseus unlocked the gates of Troy and opened them wide.
There stood the rest of the Greek warriors. Their eyes
reflected the fire of the torches they held. The entire fleet had
returned after dark and had silently come ashore again. Now
they poured in through the open gates—the gates that had
kept them out for ten years.

They ran in every direction, setting buildings ablaze. The sleepy Trojans awoke from peaceful dreams and found themselves in a fiery nightmare. Everywhere they looked, the city was burning. Greek warriors swarmed through the streets. Along the top of the Trojan wall were the shadows of still more Greeks.

The Trojans scrambled about, searching for helmets, shields, and swords. Some of them were cut down before they could arm themselves. Others managed to find spears or knives, and they did their best to defend themselves. But there was no time to form a plan of battle. The Greeks swept through the city.

King Priam and Queen Hecuba knew that there was no hope of saving their city. They fled to the temple of Zeus, in the inner courtyard of their palace. But the Greeks broke down the front door and quickly surrounded them. Priam was killed, and Hecuba was taken captive.

All the Trojan heroes except one were killed before the night was over. The surviving Trojan was Aeneas—the son of Aphrodite. He had fought bravely to defend his home, but now he knew there was no hope for Troy. So Aphrodite led him safely through the burning streets and out the gates.

Unseen by the Greeks, Aeneas made his way to a nearby hill. From there, he looked down on a city in flames. The walls and ancient towers crumbled and tumbled in. By morning, there was nothing left but the smoking ruins of a once-great city. Troy had fallen.

And what of the lovely Helen, for whom the Trojan War had
been fought? She, too, was led out of the city by Aphrodite
—the very goddess who had made her go away with Paris so
many years ago. Now she was reunited with her husband,
Menelaos. And together, they set sail for their distant home-
land of Sparta.